*The tour of the castle in this book is divided
into four sections featuring different parts of
the castle. You can follow them in any order.*

INTRODUCTION

*C*rowning its hilltop south of [...] looks every inch the great medieval and later fortress that it is. For around six centuries, it was the key defensive point on the Isle of Wight. Because of the island's location, this meant that it was also of enormous significance in the defence of the realm. But like all castles, it was not just for defence. It was also the centre of a great barony, the seat of its court and treasury and the principal residence of its lord.

The hilltop had been used long before the Norman conquest and the foundation of the castle. In the sixth century AD it was the site of an Anglo-Saxon cemetery and around AD1000 it probably became the site of an English defensive work against Danish raids.

After the Norman conquest in 1066, this earlier work became the basis of the first Norman castle on the island. This was replaced by the present castle, with its massive earthworks, around 1100 when the island was granted to the de Redvers family. For nearly 200 years it was the seat of this great barony, passing in 1293 to the crown.

*The seal of George Carey,
captain of the castle under
Elizabeth I*

The focus of the castle's use became more defensive as southern England became more vulnerable to the threat of French and then Spanish invasion in late medieval and Tudor times. Because of this, Carisbrooke retained its defensive role much longer than most medieval castles. In the 1590s, it was one of the very few places to be wholly refortified under Queen Elizabeth I, with a new perimeter nearly a mile long.

In the seventeenth century Carisbrooke housed its most famous, if unwilling, resident, Charles I, who was imprisoned here in 1647–8. Although Carisbrooke then faded from the national stage, its ceremonial role as the

residence of the governor of the Isle of Wight has continued almost to the present day.

*Charles I in the castle
during his imprisonment,
from a contemporary
royalist print*

THE LAYOUT OF THE CASTLE

The medieval castle took its present overall shape around 1100 when the earthworks of the motte (tall mound) and bailey (enclosure) were built. It is roughly rectangular with the motte in the north-east corner. The stone defences on top of the banks and mound were built before 1136. The interior took much longer to reach its present form and has been subject to continual changes for over 900 years to meet the needs of its users. Gradually though, in the early medieval period, particular functions became fixed in various parts of the castle and have remained so since.

From the wall-walk by the gatehouse, you can see four groups of buildings. Immediately in front of you is the Chapel of St Nicholas. Along the north curtain wall (to your left) and projecting from it are the Great Hall and its associated buildings. Behind them, on top of the mound, is the keep. Finally, to the right of the keep is an L-shaped range of buildings. The garden walls dividing up the bailey into four distinct areas are probably the latest (eighteenth-century) addition to the castle plan.

The earliest function to become fixed was probably the Chapel of St Nicholas. This was founded in the eleventh century and the chapel has been on the same site ever since. In the twelfth century, we know of two domestic buildings, one under the present hall and one opposite it now under the main lawn. There must have been others but these have not yet been found.

The main elements of the present interior plan took shape during the time of Countess Isabella (1262–93). She built or rebuilt the Great Hall on its present site and added other domestic accommodation at either end of it. The principal buildings of the castle have been here ever since. This was where the lords of the castle lived and where the main ceremonial and administrative functions were performed. Some of the buildings are still recognisably those built by Isabella. Others have been totally rebuilt or even demolished.

The buildings in the south-east corner of the castle to the right of the keep look Victorian, but began life in the fourteenth century. They have probably always been service buildings, providing workshop and storage space or accommodation for officials and garrison. Other accommodation would have been provided around the castle in the gatehouse itself, in the keep and wall towers, and in other buildings now lost.

The interior of the castle from the wall-walk, looking over the Chapel of St Nicholas towards the Great Hall and keep beyond

MEDIEVAL DEFENCES

This tour takes you on a complete circuit of the medieval castle walls, and includes the medieval keep. It gives good views over the castle defences as well as the interior of the castle.

SOUTHERN WALL-WALK

From the guardhouse, cross the courtyard and climb the stairway in the corner, to the right of the gatehouse. Turn left, to follow the wall-walk in an anti-clockwise direction. This spot by the gatehouse is a good place from which to appreciate the whole interior of the castle (see box opposite).

Looking out from the walls, it is easy to appreciate the castle's superb defensive position on its hilltop. Close at hand the ground slopes steeply down on all sides except the east. At the foot of the hill on this, western, side of the castle is the Clatterford valley. Here, probably, was the settlement that preceded the first fortification of the hilltop. On a clear day, you can see deep into the interior of the island.

These walls existed by 1136 but their tops have frequently been modified since. There is a good view of the flat roof of the gatehouse, itself a fighting platform for the defence of the castle, and of its surviving medieval chimney. Further along this stretch of the wall-walk is the cross-shaped opening known as **Heynoe's loop**, the only surviving medieval loophole in the parapet wall.

*Walk towards the **tower** at the south-west angle.*

From the start, the builders of the castle wanted to provide flanking fire along the base of the walls to protect them from attack on all sides (except the north, which was naturally too steep for an assault). This was done by building projecting towers at the south-east and south-west corners of the defences, as well as by the gatehouse and the keep.

ABOVE: This opening, known as Heynoe's loop, enabled an archer to see and shoot at the enemy, while he was protected from their fire. It is named after a bowman who in 1377 is said to have killed the commander of French invading forces with a single shot (see page 25)

LEFT: The Norman ramparts and medieval walls on the south side of the castle, towering above the later artillery fortress

The bastion or knight at the south-west corner of the medieval defences. These knights were primitive artillery bastions built around the existing angles of the castle walls. They could carry both guns firing along the faces of the walls and also guns firing out at enemy positions

This tower was originally rectangular. Its front and side walls were built of stone and its back one of wood (now totally disappeared). The top of its surviving part can be seen on the left. Originally it was much taller than now, and covered with a coat of lime plaster.

Tall towers with sharp angles were very vulnerable to artillery and so became obsolete in the sixteenth century. In 1587, as the threat of Spanish invasion loomed, the government accounts record 'takinge downe two towers' and the building of two 'knights', projecting from the south-west and south-east corners of the castle. These primitive artillery bastions were lower than the towers they superseded and had shallow-angled corners, making them less vulnerable to enemy artillery fire.

This bastion and its companion at the south-east angle were modified in 1601 and 1602. The present parapet is nineteenth-century. Excavation has shown that the knight was in any case carelessly built so that it would probably not have withstood effective gunfire.

Continue along the south side of the defences.

There are excellent views from this stretch of the wall-walk both of the castle interior and down on to the long, low banks and ditches of the artillery defences thrown around the castle between 1597 and 1602. (*To tour the artillery defences, see page 10.*)

Halfway along this long length of wall there was a further projecting tower to strengthen it. Its side and back walls have been demolished and its front wall reduced to the height of the rest of the curtain wall. At the **south-east corner**, the sequence seen already at the south-west corner is repeated. Notice how the wall of the knight of 1587 has been thickened internally to provide greater strength.

The **eastern side** of the medieval defences is complicated. The banks surrounding the original bailey, onto which the curtain wall was built, terminated in a small mound, set on the edge of the ditch which went right round the motte and cut it off from the rest of the castle. This small mound (or counter-motte) had a tower on its top to strengthen the defences of the ditch. That tower has long gone and the shape of the counter-motte has been obscured by the buildings and yards cut into it from the fourteenth century.

The curtain wall across this mound is missing, and the path crosses a wooden bridge to a further stretch of curtain wall blocking the motte ditch. This wall was built in the fourteenth century when the defences of this part of the castle were re-shaped. A small tower was built on one edge of the ditch to protect the new stretch of wall. Originally the curtain wall continued up the motte from this tower to link up with the keep wall.

Looking out from this stretch of wall, there is a good view of the Bowling Green created for Charles I during his imprisonment here (*see page 10*).

Go down the stair on the far side of the little tower. From here, either turn left and out through the postern gate to see the Bowling Green and the artillery defences (*see page 9*); or turn right to continue the tour of the medieval defences. From the tower, follow the path round the edge of the **motte ditch**. Originally, this ditch was at least 4 metres deeper than now, and much wider. The building to the left is in fact built over the original side of the ditch. The arches at the base of its wall are relieving arches founded on piers that go down through the ditch fill to solid chalk, to provide the building with firm foundations.

This tower on the edge of the motte ditch was added in the fourteenth century to improve the defences on the eastern side of the castle

KEEP

*On the right is the **motte** itself, the ultimate stronghold within the castle. Climb the motte by the stone steps (there are 71) next to the north curtain wall. At the top of the motte is the keep.*

The keep was the last refuge of the defenders of the castle. In many castles, particularly royal ones such as Dover or the Tower of London, the keep was a great stone tower which could also provide sumptuous accommodation for the castle's lord. It was not possible to build such towers on man-made mounds for reasons of stability, particularly in the decades immediately after the motte's construction.

An alternative approach was to build a so-called shell-keep around the top of the motte. This was simply a relatively low enclosing wall, since the mound itself added greatly to its

The motte, built c.1100, crowned by the twelfth-century keep. The gatehouse was added in about 1335

RIGHT: The motte at Carisbrooke was built of alternating horizontal layers of loose and rammed chalk above a base layer of angular flints. This gave stability to the structure and follows the practice shown here in the Bayeux Tapestry

BELOW: The keep gate passage, added about 1335

FAR RIGHT: The garderobe in the keep would originally have emptied over the outer side of the motte. Remains of its stone seat survive

BELOW: The well in the keep is 48 metres deep and may be the one which ran dry in 1136 (see page 22)

RIGHT: View of the keep interior looking south-west towards the centre of the Isle of Wight

defensive strength. Single-storey lean-to buildings were constructed against the interior face of this surrounding wall. With some notable exceptions, shell-keeps tended to be cramped and did not contain the principal accommodation of the castle.

The original keep at Carisbrooke would have been of wood. Its form is not known. By 1136 there was a stone fortification on the motte. This must have been the present shell-keep, though what can now be seen has been greatly modified. It was probably higher than it is now. At the top of the stairs is a small gatehouse added around 1335. It is vaulted to lessen the risk of fire and has a portcullis groove in the outside arch. The roof of the tower would have been a fighting platform. It has been massively buttressed to give it stability on the side of the motte.

From the gatehouse, follow the narrow passage into the centre of the keep.

The walls inside the keep are sixteenth-century additions, but the two fireplaces set back to back are remains of an earlier arrangement, as is the garderobe (lavatory) set into the surrounding wall of the keep. In the room on the left of the entrance passage is one of the two castle wells. Traces of the support for its timber windlass can be seen in the adjoining wall.

The views from the top of the keep wall are spectacular. On a clear day, it is possible to see the Solent and across to the mainland. On the far side of the keep, above the ground-floor garderobe, is the shaft of another which once existed at this higher level.

NORTHERN WALL-WALK

Go down the stairway from the keep. Do not go all the way to ground level but veer to the right onto the northern wall-walk.

Looking outwards, there is a good view of Carisbrooke village, the medieval settlement associated with the castle. The village runs down a ridge on the opposite side of the valley from the castle. The most prominent building is the medieval parish church. In the valley bottom is the restored Carisbrooke millpond.

The northern wall-walk runs alongside the principal domestic buildings of the castle (*see page 14*). The roofed building immediately on the left is the Great Hall. Between it and the wall-walk are the ruins of a two-storey block which joined the hall to the curtain wall, and beyond are the ruins of Carey's Mansion, built by George Carey, governor of the island from 1582 to 1602.

At the end of the northern wall-walk, return to ground level by the same stairway which you climbed up.

The north wall-walk

OUTER DEFENCES

Carisbrooke is not just a medieval castle. It succeeded an earlier defensive circuit, probably dating to around 1000. In the late sixteenth century, the medieval castle was absorbed into a modern artillery fortress. Both fortifications show the importance of this hilltop in the defence of the Isle of Wight. To see them, leave the medieval castle through the postern or side gate in the eastern defences next to the motte.

EARLY DEFENCES: THE LOWER ENCLOSURE

Follow the footpath across the castle ditch and walk into the middle of the Bowling Green. Then turn round and look back at the medieval castle.

To the right is the motte, crowned by its keep, and to the left are the earthworks of the bailey bank. In the middle is the curtain wall blocking the motte ditch where it passed through the castle defences. At the base of the earthworks, stretches of a low wall are intermittently visible, with an apparent break where the two ends of the wall curve back under the bailey bank.

Stretches of this wall have been traced at the base of the bailey bank not just here, but also on the other sides of the castle. It was discovered after World War I when the ramparts were returfed. Surrounding what is now known as the Lower Enclosure, it was built as the front to an earlier earth bank and was itself of two successive periods. Generally, the bottom courses of the wall are built of large stones. The only known entrance is here, where the two walls curve back under the later bailey bank. The apparent inner end of a long entrance passage has been found under the building now containing the exhibition.

Excavation suggests that the Lower Enclosure is most likely to date from around 1000. If so, it is one of many fortified places built across southern England in the tenth and eleventh centuries to protect against Viking raids. The Isle of Wight was raided several times by the Danes in this period.

ABOVE: The Lower Enclosure wall, cut away by the motte ditch and overridden by the fourteenth-century wall blocking the ditch

LEFT: The Lower Enclosure entrance (foreground). This is the best preserved stretch of the Lower Enclosure wall and seems to have been built to the highest standard, with well-shaped rectangular blocks

OPPOSITE: View over the north ramparts, looking north-east across Newport towards the Solent and mainland

The Bowling Green was constructed for Charles I inside earlier fortifications

The artillery defences on the south side of the castle. Long low banks and ditches were faced with stone walls to provide maximum protection against gunfire

BOWLING GREEN

The Bowling Green is surrounded by massive terraced banks, with small artillery bastions at the far corners. Originally this earthwork was an additional defence for the castle, probably belonging to the work done in 1587. The terracing of the banks probably dates from the conversion of this space into a bowling green for Charles I's recreation during his captivity here in 1648.

ARTILLERY DEFENCES

Cross the Bowling Green diagonally to the far right corner and walk up to the small angle bastion. The cannon here and on the matching bastion are nineteenth-century naval guns given to the castle early in the twentieth century. From the outer tip of this bastion, walk down to the latest fortifications of the castle.

The threat of a further Spanish invasion in 1597 persuaded Queen Elizabeth to agree to the creation of an artillery fortress around the medieval castle. A new rampart and ditch, nearly a mile long, were built with large projecting bastions at the four corners and an additional bastion in the middle of the west side to protect the entrance to the fortress. These earthworks were faced with stone walls for maximum protection against gunfire. Their designer, an Italian engineer called Federigo Gianibelli, was clearly worried by the comparative vulnerability of the south and east sides of the defences and made the bastions on these sides particularly strong.

Turn right and walk south along the rampart.

Looking along this, it is easy to see how the ditch would have been protected by the bastions at either end. At the end of the Bowling Green, you can turn right and walk back up on to it and so return to the main part of the castle.

Alternatively, continue walking along the rampart of the artillery fortress to the next bastion. To the right, the towering banks and walls of the medieval castle must have appeared very formidable to an attacker. At either end are the two earlier knights or bastions added to the medieval curtain wall in 1587 and modified in 1601–2. If the light is right, you can make out the date 1601 carved on a stone on one knight and 1602 on the other.

The **flanker battery** at the west end of this stretch of rampart has been fully excavated. The recessed front wall of the battery is protected by the flanking projection of the bastion. Only the lower part of this front wall, including the doorway, is original. Inside the battery, the excavations have been filled in to protect the fragile remains, but its principal features are still clear. To one side, and separated from the battery by a wall, a passage led down to the sally port or side entrance. The low bank at the front of the battery covers its original front wall. Two guns on the lower level fired directly over the top of this wall. The low mound at the centre covers a masonry pier which supported the upper deck of the battery on a brick vault. The front of the upper deck was in line with the front of this pier. This would have allowed smoke to clear from the

guns on the lower deck but might have put them at risk from sparks and debris from the guns on the upper level.

These elaborate batteries seem to have been used for only a short time. This one was probably demolished and filled in some time not long after 1620, except for the passage down to the sally port.

To continue the tour, retrace your steps along the rampart. Turn left into the gap between the medieval castle and the Bowling Green and then return into the medieval castle through the postern gate.

The south-west flanker battery, which held guns on two levels to fire along the face of the rampart

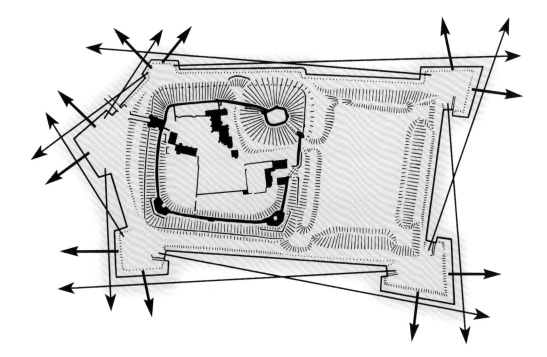

At the corners of the artillery defences, large arrowhead bastions were equipped to cover the whole perimeter of the castle. Their outward facing sides carried batteries of guns to shoot at enemy positions. On their short flanks, there were batteries to sweep the defences themselves with fire. On the east and south sides, these were of two storeys to give extra protection to these more vulnerable areas

CASTLE INTERIOR

Castles were not solely defensive in the middle ages. They were also the homes of great lords. As such they had to provide accommodation befitting the lord's rank, demonstrate his or her status to the rest of the world through their grandeur, and fulfil a number of administrative functions. Even on the military level, castles housed garrisons, stored supplies and so forth. Unusually, Carisbrooke retained its military role well into the seventeenth century because of the front line position of the Isle of Wight. It retained its role as the residence of the governor of the Isle of Wight until 1944 and still has a significant ceremonial function in the island.

Over the centuries the castle has contained buildings for all these roles: some have been demolished while others have been added. All that survive have been adapted through successive generations either to fulfil new roles or to meet the changing needs and fashions of existing ones. At times, there was much more accommodation inside the castle than there is now. Nearly all the present buildings contain fabric dating back to the medieval period.

CHAPEL OF ST NICHOLAS

The Chapel of St Nicholas, still a parish church in its own right, existed by 1086 since it is recorded in Domesday Book. It is the only building in the castle that can be traced back before the construction of the motte-and-bailey castle around 1100. No masonry of that period is now visible since the chapel has been rebuilt several times. The present chapel stands on thirteenth-century foundations, of which the footings (foundations) of the buttresses are visible, but was built only in 1904. It replaced the chapel dismantled in 1856, which itself was built in 1738 to replace a medieval chapel.

The new building, designed by Percy Stone, was meant to mark the 250th anniversary of Charles I's execution. It is a rectangular building with a late medieval feel to its rather plain exterior. The porch at the west end of the north

ABOVE: The bust of Charles I by Bernini, in the ante-chapel

LEFT: The chapel after it was dismantled in 1856 and before its rebuilding in 1904

OPPOSITE: The chapel interior looking east. The chapel serves as the island's war memorial and the woodwork came from HMS Nettle, one of the last wooden warships

The statues around the altar represent the patron saints of all the island churches

Exterior of the hall and chamber block, looking east

wall leads into a small ante-chapel, dominated by Bernini's bust of Charles I. The organ was given by Edward VII and came from the Rolls Chapel in Chancery Lane. The richly decorated interior is in marked contrast to the exterior. This was not part of the original concept but reflects the decision after World War I that the church should be the Isle of Wight war memorial. The names of the 2000 men from the island who were killed in both world wars are inscribed on the stone panels between the windows. The altar painting was commissioned by Princess Beatrice (*see page 31*) in memory of her son Maurice, killed at Ypres in 1914.

GREAT HALL: EXTERIOR

Cross the courtyard to the Great Hall.

The complex of buildings in front of you provided the principal domestic accommodation of the castle for over 700 years, down to 1949. As a result it has undergone many alterations over the years to meet the changing tastes and needs of successive occupiers.

The long two-storey building is the Great Hall itself. There was a small twelfth-century building here whose undercroft still provides the cellar under part of the present hall. However, one surviving window shows the present hall to be in origin thirteenth-century and built either by Countess Isabella, who held the castle from 1262 to 1293, or one of her immediate predecessors.

In the middle ages the hall was the heart of the castle. Most people ate here. It was the focus for the castle's administrative and ceremonial functions, and for the government of the whole island. Between the hall and the curtain wall

would have been the kitchens and other offices, now ruinous, needed for feeding a great household. At either end of the hall there were also chambers providing more private accommodation for the lord and his family. Isabella built on to the hall extensively, adding chambers at both ends and the small Chapel of St Peter projecting from its east side. The three-storey block to the right of the hall, known as the **Constable's Lodging**, is the work of William de Montacute, Earl of Salisbury, who added it in 1397. This contained the great chamber and other apartments. The other buildings are later.

Between 1584 and 1586 George Carey carried out the most drastic alterations to the hall. As well as adding Carey's Mansion as a projecting wing almost as large as the hall itself, he raised the roof of the hall and inserted an upper floor, thereby creating its present overall appearance. The present, medieval-style windows of the Constable's Lodging replaced sash windows during a restoration in the mid-nineteenth century while the main windows of the hall are even later, installed only in 1901, the same year as the construction of the flat-roofed extension.

GREAT HALL: INTERIOR

Enter the Great Hall through the porch at its north-west corner.

Originally, this porch continued across the hall as a screens passage, dividing the hall proper, on the right, from service rooms and the passage to the kitchens on the left. It now opens into the ground floor of the present hall. Despite its generally

ancient appearance, the room is a mixture of many periods. The hall now houses the **Carisbrooke Castle Museum**, whose collection includes memorabilia relating to Charles I.

Originally the hall would have been open to the roof. The far end would have been the upper end with a dais at which the lord would have eaten on special occasions. The fourteenth-century doorway and blocked stair in the end wall originally led into the lord's private apartments beyond. (This part of the building is used by the museum and is not normally open to the public.) The hall was lit by

pairs of lancet (pointed arched) windows, one of which was discovered in 1856 behind the magnificent later fireplace inserted by William de Montacute.

The present character of the room reflects the drastic alterations to the hall by George Carey in the 1580s. The ceiling results from his insertion of an upper floor to provide more accommodation.

Beyond the fireplace, a doorway leads into the former **Chapel of St Peter**, now occupied by the staircase to the upper floor. Originally, this was the private chapel built by Countess Isabella around 1270, an elegant room with arcades on the walls and lancet windows. You can still see the thin rectangular squint – an oblique cut in

A lady and her maid, from the fourteenth-century Luttrell Psalter

BRITISH LIBRARY (ADD. 42130 F. 63)

FAR LEFT: *Charles I attempted his first escape from Carisbrooke (see page 29) through the window of his bedchamber, which was on the first floor of the Constable's Lodging. This window replaced it in 1856*

LEFT: *William de Montacute's fine fireplace blocked the lancet windows, dating from Isabella's time, behind it. Previously the hall was probably heated by a fire in the centre of the room from which smoke would have escaped through a hole in the roof*

The sixteenth-century Carisbrooke Parish Gun, inside the porch of the Great Hall. Each parish on the island was provided with one as a means of defence against invasion

ABOVE: *By Isabella's time, the wealthy were seeking greater privacy and creating chambers for their personal use. This window in the north wall (blocked during the wars with France) was in her great chamber, and had window seats overlooking the valley. Her accounts show that it was glazed, a great luxury at the time*

RIGHT: *Carey's Mansion, seen from the wall-walk*

the wall – by the southern window, which allowed the countess to see and take part in the service while remaining in her private apartment. In the sixteenth century, George Carey inserted an upper floor and in about 1692 the then governor, Lord Cutts, removed the upper floor, inserted the staircase and panelled the walls. The remains of the chapel were only rediscovered in 1856 when restoration works were carried out.

Carey's **upper floor** remains close to its original form. He partitioned it into two rooms, both with fireplaces, and leading into small rooms at the far end of the hall. It was on this floor that Charles I whiled away much of his imprisonment, and the left-hand room is where his daughter Princess Elizabeth is thought to have died at the age of 14 in 1650. Her room is displayed by the Carisbrooke Castle Museum as it might have been at the time of her death.

NORTH RANGE

Leave the hall through the door by which you entered and turn right.

Beside the hall is **Carey's Mansion**, built between 1584 and 1586 to provide accommodation fit for Carey's status as governor of the island and cousin to Elizabeth I. Arranged around a central stair, the mansion was of two storeys and originally had 13 chambers. The building's façade to the main courtyard would have been impressive with the central entrance flanked by large bay windows.

Use the steps between Carey's Mansion and the west curtain wall to reach the first floor of Carey's Mansion, and continue behind this into the ruins of the rooms which formerly lay between the hall and the castle wall.

This space was originally another of Countess Isabella's private chambers. Since then this area has been heavily altered several times. In Carey's time it was turned into kitchens and service rooms with bedrooms above. The fireplaces and oven date from this time. It was from one of the windows in this area that Charles I made his second escape attempt.

*Continue past the hall block and down the steps into the courtyard, then turn right past the hall until you come to the **wellhouse**. This is the small detached building constructed over the castle well (see box opposite).*

SOUTH-EAST CORNER

Beyond the wellhouse and through the archway is a group of buildings in the south-east corner of the castle. Although they now look like nineteenth-century buildings, excavation and analysis have shown that they date back to the fourteenth century. Originally an L-shaped range of buildings was built around the so-called counter-motte, thus explaining the high level courtyard behind them which was part of that earthwork. The building facing you opposite the archway was built over the edge of the motte ditch (*see page 4*). At a later date the courtyard and outbuildings were added in front of this complex. On the bank in front of the yard wall is a small battery of saluting cannon.

These buildings have had many functions over the years. In the nineteenth century they housed the Isle of Wight militia and later accommodation for Princess Beatrice's staff – a tunnel led from them to the hall block. They also housed coaches. The Coach House now contains an exhibition on the history of the castle as well as a tea room. One of the outbuildings houses the Donkey Centre while another is the castle fire station.

Leave the yard by the entrance next to the fire station.

In the garden beyond is a small underground magazine for gunpowder, probably re-used as an ice-house in the nineteenth century. Beyond this garden is Princess Beatrice's garden and from there it is possible to retrace your steps to the main courtyard.

The underground powder magazine

THE CASTLE'S WELLS

A donkey demonstrates the use of the treadwheel

A secure water supply is an essential part of any castle. Failure of the water supply, as happened at Carisbrooke in 1136, could only lead to the surrender of the castle.

Carisbrooke has two wells. One in the keep is now dry and may be the one that failed in 1136. The second lies in the courtyard to the south of the Great Hall in its own wellhouse. The well itself is 49m (161ft) deep, the upper part lined with masonry and the lower part cut through chalk. It still contains water to a depth of about 12m (40ft).

There was certainly a wellhouse with a treadwheel to raise the water in the time of Countess Isabella. Repairs are recorded in 1292 and again in 1334 when a rope 35 fathoms (180ft) long was bought.

The present wellhouse and treadwheel were built by George Carey as part of the improvements made in 1587. This treadwheel has remained in use ever since, although from the early twentieth century, when the castle was put on mains water, this has been for demonstration to visitors only.

Originally the wheel must have been worked by prisoners. The first recorded use of any other source of motive power is the observation of the famous traveller Celia Fiennes in 1696 that water was drawn by a 'horse' or 'ass'. From then on donkeys seem to have been used, although until 1880 only one was kept at the castle. Now a team of donkeys shares the work. Their training takes about seven months and they work for only two hours a day to demonstrate the use of the wheel. You can find out more about the donkeys' history and lives at Carisbrooke in the Donkey Centre, through the archway beyond the wellhouse.

This engraving of 1865 shows visitors being offered samples of the well water

GATEHOUSE

Entrances to castles were always potential weak points in their defence. They tended therefore to be heavily fortified. Often, too, they provided high-class accommodation for one of the senior officials of the castle, normally the constable who commanded it in the absence of its lord.

EXTERIOR

The principal and, originally, only entrance to Carisbrooke Castle has been on the same spot since at least 1100. For the best view of the gatehouse turn left out of the ticket office, walk right through the gatehouse passage and across the bridge. Beyond is a second bridge with an Elizabethan gate at its inner end. You can see Elizabeth I's initial and the date 1598 on the pediment. This gate marks the entry to the castle through the artillery defences built around it between 1597 and 1601. To either side are flanking bastions from which cannon could sweep the entry point with fire.

The gate passage, showing the portcullis slots. The small door leads via a passage into a guard room on the ground floor of the drum tower – there is a similar arrangement on the other side

The medieval gateway was a tower, fronted by a deep ditch. This was crossed via a drawbridge, which was replaced by a masonry bridge in the sixteenth century. No trace remains of the original tower, which would have been wooden. By the late thirteenth century the gatehouse was a square stone tower over the gate passage. The round projecting drum towers were added in 1335–6. They were heightened in 1378 and modified again around 1470. Linked by a projecting fighting platform with machicolations – holes through which missiles could be dropped on an attacker – the towers provided extra protection. These towers have both cross-shaped slits for bowmen, and loopholes shaped like inverted key-holes for early handguns.

GATE PASSAGE

The gate passage contains three portcullis slots, which are matched below ground by the filled-in pits of successive drawbridges marking the successive enlargements of the gatehouse. There are gates at both ends of the gate passage. Those at the inner end are medieval, while the outer gates date to 1897 when the whole gatehouse was restored.

INTERIOR

To reach the upper floors of the gatehouse, return through the gate passage and climb the outside stairs on your right as you enter the courtyard.

These steps lead up to a doorway and small lobby at first-floor level. The doorway on the right, now blocked by a grille, leads to a flight of stairs in the thickness of the wall. This once led to the second floor of the gatehouse.

The other doorway enters the first-floor chamber. This is now double its original height since its ceiling was not replaced when the gatehouse was restored. To the right is a fireplace and to the left was the entrance to a small chamber, probably a garderobe (lavatory). The presence of the fireplace and garderobe shows that this was once accommodation for someone important. The fireplace at an upper level belongs to the second floor of the gatehouse.

The gatehouse was restored in 1897 as a memorial to Prince Henry Maurice of Battenberg, governor and captain of the Isle of Wight and husband to Princess Beatrice, the youngest daughter of Queen Victoria. After that, the gatehouse was used as the Carisbrooke Castle Museum until it was moved to the hall in 1949.

The doorway at the front of the chamber leads through to the drum towers. The medieval arrangements here are unclear. To the right, the first floor of the northern drum tower contains a good example of a loophole for bowmen. The iron spiral stair in the south tower leads back down to the gate passage.

ABOVE: *The fireplace in the first-floor chamber of the gatehouse. The inscription above it commemorates Prince Henry of Battenberg, who died on active service in 1896 during the Ashanti War in west Africa*

LEFT: *The gatehouse. The drum towers were cylindrical because corners were more vulnerable to undermining and missiles. The inverted key shaped openings are loopholes for handguns*

netley · S Andros · Iychesfilde

PPP PPP PPP

Rowner · gosport

heathe

Calshard·

stoke

haselborde

falley

stoke bay

the brables

Bewley·

West cow · est cow · Meadehole · Showflyt Wottō hauon · sandc hed

gurner · Whytozhamll · park · quar

blackberg · north wood · Ryde · nettellstone

parkehurst · Ashe · mialest · S Elly

shoflyt · newton · Worsley

colburne · Newport · Areton

thurley · the kyngs pke · Casebroke · newchurch · Bradynge

swenston · VECTA Gacu Wyght·

freshe wat · Shorewell · Godshytt · Bitbryg · yauland

Rowner · bmoke · Dynney · kyngston

Motfirt · brykston · Whytwell · Apledor Coumbe

S Woluton · worsley · Sanden bay·

freshe wat bay· · Compto bay · chale · Chynkly · Chynkyng chyne·

Chale bay· · S kataryne S laurens · S Bonifac

Dounose·

20

HISTORY OF THE CASTLE

The Isle of Wight lies astride one of the main invasion routes into southern England. At times of war – such as the Danish invasions of the tenth and eleventh centuries and the conflicts with France and then Spain in late medieval and Tudor times – it has been particularly vulnerable to attack. For much of this time, from around AD1000 to the mid-seventeenth century, Carisbrooke was the major place of defence and centre of authority on the island.

BEFORE THE CASTLE

The area around Carisbrooke and Newport, here at the centre of the island, lies around the junction of two major communication routes: the north–south Medina river valley and the chalk ridge that runs across the island from east to west. It was an obvious focal point for wealth and power long before insecurity drove its occupants up onto the hill where the castle now stands. In the Roman period, there were two villas in the Clatterford valley, west of the castle hill, and another under Newport itself. Such a concentration indicates considerable wealth in this small area.

The earliest use of the castle hill itself was in the sixth century when it was the site of a small Anglo-Saxon cemetery. Three graves were discovered during excavations. One of them was a young man aged between 20 and 25. He had been buried with a gold coin from southern France in his mouth, together with a glass drinking bowl, a drinking horn, a large bronze bowl and a bucket. Across his lower legs were over 50 ivory counters. Three of these objects were from northern France. Such an exceptional collection clearly belonged to someone of great importance. While he did not live on the hilltop, he must have lived somewhere close by.

In the following centuries there was a major Anglo-Saxon site in the valley west of the castle which has produced evidence for trade and wide contacts.

Occupation only began on the hilltop at the time of the Viking raids. The Danes first raided the island in 896. Between 998 and 1009 they regularly based themselves on the island for raiding and invading the mainland. Around this time the kings of Wessex were fortifying the whole of their kingdom with burhs, fortified places which acted as places of refuge and defence. It is very probable that the first fortification of the hilltop, the so-called Lower Enclosure, was the burh for the Isle of Wight.

Once the centre of power had moved up to the hilltop, it remained there for many centuries.

ABOVE: Bronze fittings from a wooden bucket found in an Anglo-Saxon grave on the castle hill

OPPOSITE: The Vecta Wyght *map of 1593, showing Carisbrooke Castle at the centre of the island*

LEFT: In the tenth century the hilltop was defended by a rectangular ditch and bank, soon faced with the stone wall now visible in the bank below the medieval walls. Excavation has found large timber buildings inside

The late Saxon enclosure

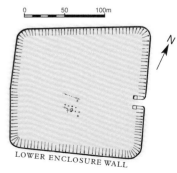

THE CASTLE OF THE CONQUEST

Following the Battle of Hastings in 1066, one of William the Conqueror's most urgent priorities was to secure the boundaries of his new kingdom against further foreign invasions. He did this in part through granting large and powerful baronies in such areas to his most loyal supporters. Along with the Rapes of Sussex, such a barony on the Isle of Wight protected the south coast.

William Fitz Osbern, the new lord of Wight, would have needed to create a secure stronghold on the island as soon as possible. The castle at Carisbrooke is recorded in Domesday Book in 1086 but was probably first built immediately after the conquest in 1066. Nothing can now be seen of that first castle, but we know from excavation that the Saxon burh was adapted to provide it. Deep ditches were dug inside the Lower Enclosure to create a secure rectangular inner bailey in its north-east quadrant. The remainder of the enclosure would have been the outer bailey of the castle, with a gateway on the site of the present gatehouse and the Chapel of St Nicholas (which also existed by 1086) on its present site.

William's lordship was short-lived. He was killed in battle in 1071 and his heir, Roger, was deprived of all his lands for treason five years after that. Carisbrooke and the Isle of Wight then remained in the hands of the crown until 1100 when the whole was granted to Richard de Redvers.

THE CASTLE OF THE DE REDVERS

Henry I had seized the throne in 1100 on the death of William Rufus by *coup de main* from his elder brother Robert. At the beginning of his reign, he needed to secure and reward the loyalty of his supporters and also to prevent invasion from Normandy, still held by Robert until 1106. Richard de Redvers was therefore built up into a great magnate with extensive estates both in Devon and on the Isle of Wight.

It was probably Richard who built the great motte-and-bailey castle which has shaped all subsequent developments at Carisbrooke. The castle constructed in haste after the Norman conquest would have needed updating. More importantly, Richard would have needed to demonstrate his new powers and position to his vassals and his peers. The new and massive earthworks at Carisbrooke, and the buildings inside, would have left little doubt in anybody's mind about his status and power.

Richard had died by 1107 and it must have been his son, Baldwin, who replaced the initial timber defences with the stone curtain wall, towers and keep that crown the earthworks. In 1136, the strength of the castle seemed likely to be tested when Baldwin took the side of Henry I's daughter Matilda, when she contested the decision to place Stephen, Henry's nephew, on the throne. However, failure of the well meant that Baldwin was forced to surrender to Stephen at Southampton.

Their lands restored to them after 1153, a succession of de Redvers lords then held Carisbrooke. Little is known of how the castle developed until the rule of the last of these, Countess Isabella de Fortibus. Immensely wealthy and mistress of the Isle of Wight for over 30 years, she chose to make Carisbrooke her principal residence, rebuilding and reshaping the interior to give us the bones of what we now see (*see box*).

A nobleman kneels to receive the sword of knighthood from a king

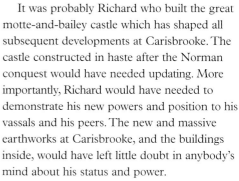

RIGHT: *The arms of the de Redvers family, rulers of the island 1100–1293*

RIGHT BELOW: *King Stephen enthroned, from an early fourteenth-century chronicle*

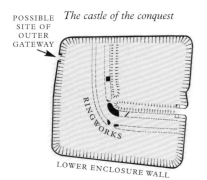

POSSIBLE SITE OF OUTER GATEWAY

The castle of the conquest

RINGWORKS

LOWER ENCLOSURE WALL

COUNTESS ISABELLA

From 1100 to 1293 the Isle of Wight was held by the de Redvers family. The last de Redvers lord of the island was in fact a woman, Countess Isabella de Fortibus. Widowed in 1260 at the age of 23, she had inherited the lands of her husband, William de Fortibus, Earl of Albemarle, which lay mainly in the north around Holderness. Two years later, her brother, Baldwin, the lord of the castle, was poisoned. She thus inherited all his lands in Devon, Hampshire, and the Isle of Wight.

This made Isabella one of the great landholders of thirteenth-century England and she retained her estates to her death in 1293. To achieve this in a masculine and often dangerous world she must have been truly formidable and of very strong character.

Carisbrooke became the centre for all her estates and activities. Here she maintained her principal residence, treasury and the administration of her lands. Carisbrooke was also a law court and a prison as well as a garrison and must at this time have reached its apogee as a medieval castle.

A great builder, Isabella transformed Carisbrooke into a fitting setting for her. During her tenure it must often have felt like a perpetual construction site, as buildings were altered, extended or built from scratch. Additions included the Chapel of St Peter and the countess's Great Chamber, both extensions to the hall. Other new buildings included a chamber for the constable, a kitchen, and a salting house, while many other buildings were repaired and refurbished. The building accounts also give some idea of the more ephemeral aspects of the castle. There was, for example, a herbary (herb garden) with a sundial or clock in it, and a fish tank or vivarium for keeping fish once caught.

ABOVE: A portrait of Countess Isabella, from a corbel in Christchurch Priory, Dorset

LEFT: This jug, found in the castle, was imported in Isabella's time from Gascony in southern France

BELOW: The Chapel of St Peter. Although partly obscured by the later staircase, enough survives to give some idea of its former grandeur

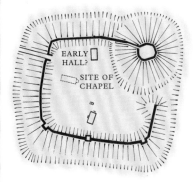

The motte-and-bailey castle

EARLY HALL?

SITE OF CHAPEL

THE LATER MEDIEVAL CASTLE

The late fourteenth-century castle

RIGHT: *William de Montacute added this chamber block at the south end of the hall. His coat of arms can be seen on the corner buttress at first-floor level*

Reconstruction of the castle as it might have looked in the fourteenth century, by Peter Schofield

Just before she died in 1293 Isabella agreed to sell the castle to King Edward I, and Carisbrooke has largely remained in crown hands ever since. From time to time in the later middle ages it was granted to one great lord or another but never remained for long in any one family. This, combined with the increasing dangers of French attack during the conflict that became known as the Hundred Years' War (1337–1453), meant that the focus of Carisbrooke's use through the following centuries was primarily military, with interest in it increasing at times of high risk.

French forces raided the island or the Solent in 1336, 1338, 1340, 1342 and 1370. In 1377, the French not only landed on the island but also attempted, unsuccessfully, to capture the castle (*see box*).

The consequences of the French threat can be seen today. The drum towers of the main gatehouse were added in 1335–6 together with the little gatehouse to the keep. In 1378 the drum towers were heightened after the previous year's assault. There are many other records of spending on the castle's defences. But domestic accommodation was not entirely neglected. William de Montacute, Earl of Salisbury, who held the castle from 1386 to 1397, inserted the splendid surviving fireplace in the Great Hall and also added the chamber block (Constable's Lodging) at the south end of the hall.

THE SIEGE OF 1377

In 1377 the French landed in strength on the north coast of the island, destroyed the towns of Yarmouth and Francheville and, advancing on Carisbrooke, besieged it. More than two centuries later, Sir John Oglander (born in 1585) wrote about the siege, and provided a colourful account of the death of the French commander:

'One Peter de Heynoe came to Sir Hugh Tyrell, then Captain of the Island, and told him he would undertake with his tiller bow to kill the commander of the French, taking his time, for he had observed him how nights and mornings he came near the castle, which on leave he killed out of a loophole on the west side of the castle, and by that means brought the French to a composition to take 1000 marks to be gone.'

The surviving loophole on the west side of the castle has long been identified as 'Heynoe's loop'.

An archer with a crossbow, from a fourteenth-century manuscript

THE TUDOR CASTLE

In the early sixteenth century Henry VIII's new defence policy for the island focused on novel fortifications actually on the coast at Yarmouth, Cowes, Sandown and elsewhere. These diminished Carisbrooke's military role. Several of the captains already lived on the Isle of Wight, while others were wholly absentee, so its residential role also declined.

In the 1580s, however, the renewed threat of Spanish invasion gave Carisbrooke a new lease of life. Elizabeth I appointed her cousin, Sir George Carey, as captain of the Isle of Wight in 1582. He not only required accommodation appropriate to his status (*see box*), but also clearly believed that Carisbrooke still had a defensive role. First, in 1587 as the threat of Spanish invasion grew, he was responsible for the construction of the two 'knights' or bastions at the south-west and south-east angles of the medieval walls, as well as other fortifications. Together with the new wellhouse, these improvements cost some £470.

Carey's biggest change to Carisbrooke, though, was to transform it into an artillery fortress in the late 1590s. Following his proposal to the queen's council in 1596, at a time when it was expected that the Spanish might try to seize the Isle of Wight, designs were drawn up by the Italian engineer Federigo Gianibelli to transform the castle into a modern fortress at an estimated cost of £2500. The work was finally completed in 1601 at a much higher cost. This artillery fortification is a lasting memorial to the influence of George Carey on the castle.

The earliest known drawing of the castle (1567), from the Newport Ligger Book

This reconstruction by Peter Schofield shows the castle as it may have looked in about 1600, when the new artillery defences surrounding the medieval castle had just been built

The Spanish Armada was sighted from the Isle of Wight on the morning of 26 July 1588. Carey later described how 'this morning began a great fight between both fleets … [which] were out of sight by three in the afternoon'

GEORGE CAREY

George Carey

George Carey, later Lord Hunsdon, became captain of the Isle of Wight in 1582 at the age of 34, and remained in the post until his death in 1603. Cousin to Queen Elizabeth I, he was an important member of the ruling classes.

Clearly conscious of his position in life, one of his first priorities at Carisbrooke was to provide accommodation suitable for his status. In this he was following fashion, as all over England at this time members of the nobility were busily modernising their outdated homes. A survey in 1583 found the buildings to be in a poor state:

> '*I finde the numbr of lodginges very small for recept of the Captaynes howshold, onely two lodging chambers with chimnyes, others in want of winddows and all together wthout lyght unseeled and wthout glass…*'.

Over the following two years, he spent £750 of the queen's money, obtaining which was no mean achievement, on the building of his new mansion next to the hall, the conversion of the hall block itself and other buildings. He quickly earned a reputation as a generous host, frequently entertaining all the island gentry to lavish banquets:

> '*He would have all the gentlemen of the Island their wives also there. He was a most free man in his house-keeping, and his meat was always served up to his table with a consort of wind and still music.*'

He did not forget the servants: 'The laundry was never without a hogshead of wine and a cold pasty of venison for the maids.'

CARISBROOKE IN THE CIVIL WAR

In September 1642 the conflict between King Charles I and Parliament in England culminated in civil war. Carisbrooke's long association with the monarchy was broken after its seizure by parliamentary forces in 1642 from the Countess of Portland and a garrison of 20 men. The 4th Earl of Pembroke was appointed governor for Parliament, but unlike other castles in England Carisbrooke did not recover its defensive role in the ensuing struggles.

The 4th Earl of Pembroke, governor of Carisbrooke from 1642 until 1647

Instead it acquired a role as a royal prison. To some extent this was fortuitous, since Charles I selected it for himself and then found himself a close prisoner. After his departure in 1648, however, Parliament found it convenient to continue to use the castle as a prison. Two of Charles I's children were incarcerated here in August 1650. The 14-year-old Princess Elizabeth, a delicate child, died of complications from a chill after being caught in a shower on the Bowling Green, only a few weeks after her arrival. Her brother Henry, Duke of Gloucester, remained here in lonely captivity for nearly three years, until he joined his family in exile abroad in February 1653. Thereafter, Carisbrooke was used as a prison for dissidents against Cromwell until the Restoration of Charles II in 1660. Then the tables were turned, and the castle served the same purpose for a little while for Charles's opponents.

A Victorian illustration of Princess Elizabeth on her deathbed in 1650

After Charles I's defeat in 1646, he was kept a prisoner by Parliament at Hampton Court while they tried to agree how to deal with him. His position at this time was ambivalent since people were only gradually coming to the view that the country could be ruled without a king. However, it became clear to Charles that there was little future in remaining there.

ABOVE: Charles I at his trial in 1649, after Edward Bower (d. 1667)

BELOW: This drawing by John Livesay, dated 1798, shows the windows of the chamber block as they were when Charles made his first attempt to escape, through his bedchamber window (on the first floor)

THE ROYAL PRISONER

In November 1647, Charles escaped and travelled to Titchfield House in Hampshire. Once there, he opened negotiations with Colonel Hammond, the parliamentarian governor of the Isle of Wight but also brother to his chaplain. Presumably Charles thought that on the Isle of Wight he would be less supervised than on the mainland and better able to keep contact with his supporters.

He arrived at Carisbrooke on 22 November 1647, put himself under Hammond's protection, and was housed in the Constable's Lodging and the upper floor of the hall block. At first he was allowed considerable freedom, to the extent of riding around the island. In early 1648, however, Captain John Burley, a resident of Newport, tried to raise the people to release the king. For his pains, Burley was hung and Charles's imprisonment became stricter.

Thereafter he was confined to the castle and it was at this time that the Bowling Green was created for his use. The king, however, had clearly decided that he should try to escape. He made his first attempt on 20 March, having established links with sympathisers outside the castle. The intention was that he should climb out of his bedchamber window overlooking the courtyard, lower himself on a cord, and flee the castle. However, he had forgotten to check whether he could get through the bars on his window. When he became stuck in them, the attempt had to be abandoned.

Following this attempt to escape, he was moved to another, more secure, room in the now ruined range between the hall and the north wall. Charles made a further escape attempt on 28 May, having first loosened the bars of the window with nitric acid, and bribed the guards below. But too many people were in on the secret, and two of the guards had betrayed him. On looking out of the window, Charles saw more people below than he had expected, and stayed where he was. When Charles did finally leave the castle, on 6 September 1648, it was with the approval of Parliament to join negotiations in Newport and then by various stages to London. He was eventually executed in Whitehall on 30 January 1649.

Charles I with Colonel Hammond, his reluctant gaoler. Reputedly Hammond had wind of Charles's second escape plan, for he had visited Charles shortly before the planned time for the escape, and remarked courteously: 'I am come to take leave of your majesty, for I hear you are going away.'

LEFT: Captain John Burley

ABOVE: The head of Charles's walking stick

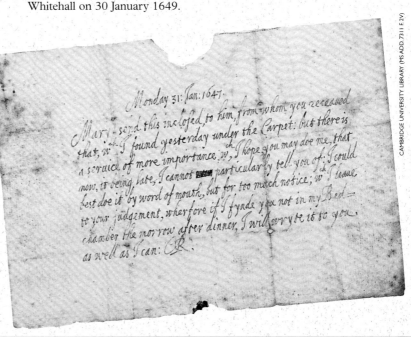

RIGHT: Charles made many plans to escape from Carisbrooke, smuggling out letters to his supporters via his chambermaid Mary. This note, dated 31 January 1648 (1647 by the old calendar), was written very early in his captivity

An engraving of the governor's house and keep in 1839, by Ackerman

LATER HISTORY

Carisbrooke never saw active service after the seventeenth century, but it retained a defensive role: it was used as a military hospital in the 1790s, and was garrisoned by batteries of the Isle of Wight artillery militia from the 1860s to the 1880s. However, it remained the official residence of the governor of the Isle of Wight. Over the ensuing two centuries much of it fell into a state of picturesque decay punctuated by occasional bursts of expenditure to render it habitable.

Lord Cutts (governor 1692–1702) renovated the governor's lodgings by removing some of the floors in the chamber block inserted by Carey and by building the present staircase through the Chapel of St Peter. In 1738 Lord Lymington replaced the medieval Chapel of St Nicholas in a modern style. This in its turn was dismantled in 1856.

During the nineteenth century, the castle came gradually to be regarded as a monument that

Engraving of the castle in 1846 by George Brannon

PERCY STONE

A long with Countess Isabella and George Carey, Percy Stone contributed greatly to the present form of the castle. He was the architect for the restoration of the gatehouse in 1897 and the chapel in 1904. He was also a historian and archaeologist, producing *The Architectural Antiquities of the Isle of Wight* in 1891. This magisterial work is still the foundation for any study of Carisbrooke Castle.

Born in London in 1856, he qualified as an architect working with his father. He moved to the Isle of Wight during the 1880s and the island became his adopted home, where he remained for the rest of his life. His architectural work focused on the repair and restoration of churches and he also built new churches in Cowes and Wootton. He designed the Island Memorial to Queen Victoria in Newport and also many war memorials.

Stone's archaeological and historical work included the excavation of Quarr Abbey as well as work at Carisbrooke and elsewhere on the island. He wrote widely about the island, both in historical works and as a poet. Under the *nom de plume* Granfer Izak, he contributed many articles in Isle of Wight dialect to the Isle of Wight County Press.

Percy Stone

PRINCESS BEATRICE

Princess Beatrice was Queen Victoria's youngest, and favourite, daughter. Born in 1857, she lived until 1944. Victoria, who spent much of her time at Osborne House on the island after Prince Albert's death, did her best to keep Beatrice close at hand. When Beatrice married Prince Henry

Princess Beatrice and her mother, Queen Victoria, in 1878

of Battenberg at Whippingham Church on the Isle of Wight in 1885, it was on condition that she and her husband continued to live at court.

Prince Henry was made governor of the Isle of Wight by his mother-in-law. In 1896 he joined the British forces in the Ashanti War in west Africa, and died of disease. Princess Beatrice succeeded him as governor, while the gatehouse of Carisbrooke Castle was restored as a memorial to him.

Prince Henry and Princess Beatrice had four children. Princess Victoria Eugenie married the King of Spain while their son, Prince Maurice, was killed at the Battle of Ypres in 1914.

Princess Beatrice restored the tradition of residence at Carisbrooke Castle by governors of the Isle of Wight. She used the castle as her summer residence from 1913 and the present form of the hall and Constable's Lodging

Princess Beatrice with her husband, Prince Henry of Battenberg

reflects this use. The buildings in the south-east corner of the castle were adapted in part for use by her staff, with a tunnel connecting them to the hall block.

The initial of Princess Beatrice on the outer gate

needed to be conserved as such. The architect Philip Hardwick carried out considerable work in 1856: for instance, he inserted medieval-style windows in the Constable's Lodging next to the hall.

The architect and antiquarian Percy Stone carried out the most sustained campaign of conservation and restoration. Following the publication of *The Architectural Antiquities of the Isle of Wight* in 1891, which contains the first and still the fullest account of the castle, Stone moved on to restore, floor and roof the gatehouse in 1897 as a memorial to Prince Henry Maurice of Battenberg, whose widow Princess Beatrice had become governor the previous year. He then restored the Chapel of St Nicholas in 1905 before fitting it out as an island war memorial after World War I.

Princess Beatrice was the last governor to use the castle as a residence. Since her death in 1944 the castle has been managed primarily as an

ancient monument and the home of the Carisbrooke Castle Museum. It still serves a ceremonial role from time to time and so preserves part of the function for which it was first built over nine centuries ago.

This photograph of the Great Hall was taken c.1900, before the replacement of the hall windows in 1901

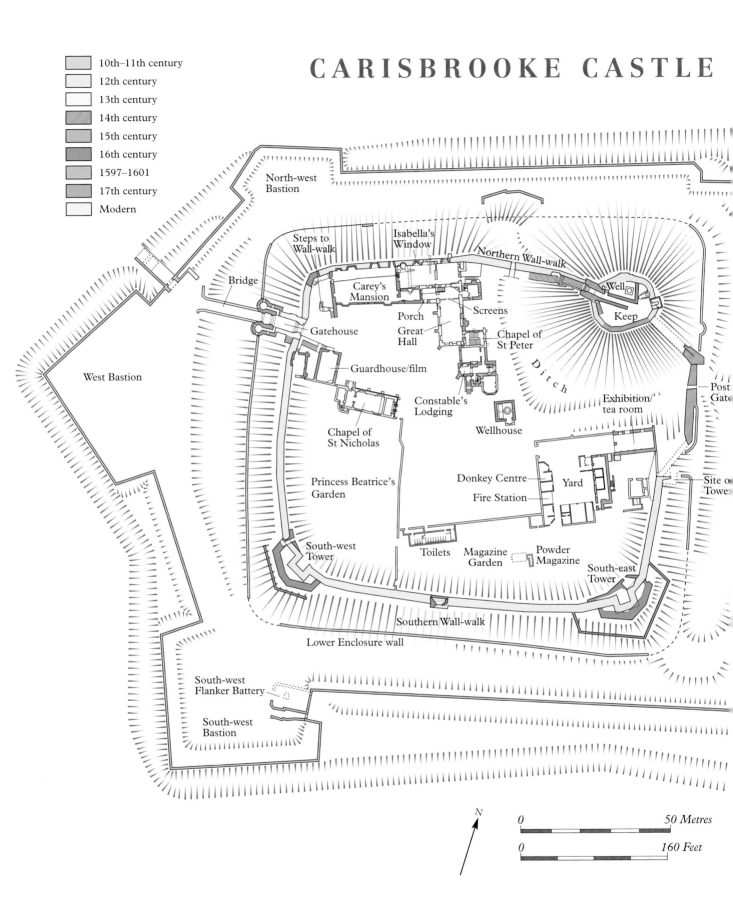

CARISBROOKE CASTLE

Legend:
- 10th–11th century
- 12th century
- 13th century
- 14th century
- 15th century
- 16th century
- 1597–1601
- 17th century
- Modern

North-west Bastion

Steps to Wall-walk

Isabella's Window

Northern Wall-walk

Bridge

Carey's Mansion

Well

Gatehouse

Porch

Screens

Keep

Great Hall

Chapel of St Peter

West Bastion

Guardhouse/film

Ditch

Constable's Lodging

Post Gate

Chapel of St Nicholas

Wellhouse

Exhibition/ tea room

Princess Beatrice's Garden

Donkey Centre

Yard

Site of Tower

Fire Station

South-west Tower

Toilets

Magazine Garden

Powder Magazine

South-east Tower

Southern Wall-walk

Lower Enclosure wall

South-west Flanker Battery

South-west Bastion

N

0   50 *Metres*

0   160 *Feet*